journey into
the desert

journey into the desert

REFLECTION AND MEDITATION FOR LENT

SUSAN SAYERS

First published in 2001 by
KEVIN MAYHEW LTD
Buxhall, Stowmarket, Suffolk IP14 3BW
E-mail: info@kevinmayhewltd.com

Scripture quotations are from:
New Revised Standard Version of the Bible, copyright
© 1989 by the Division of Christian Education of the
National Council of Churches in Christ in the USA
Used by permission. All rights reserved.

Holy Bible, New International Version. Copyright
© 1973, 1978, 1984 by International Bible Society.
Used by permission of Hodder & Stoughton Limited.
All rights reserved.

Photographs reproduced by kind permission of
Revd Andrew Ashdown, All Saints' Church,
Denmead, Hampshire.

9 8 7 6 5 4 3 2 1

ISBN 1 84003 832 2
Catalogue No. 1500466

Cover design by Angela Selfe
Edited by Katherine Laidler
Typeset by Richard Weaver

Printed and bound in Great Britain

Contents

With very special thanks to the Alternative Tourism Board who led the Nativity Trail from Nazareth to Bethlehem, and Andrew Ashdown who introduced me to the Holy Land and took the photographs.

Introduction

Jesus felt compelled to go off into the desert as he prepared for his ministry. What he encountered there was the gruelling temptation to sidestep the necessary way of love. The desert, with its space and aloneness, provided the right setting for an emerging understanding of how his saving work was to be accomplished, and its cost.

There are times when we, too, need to go off into a desert place to be with God and face up to what our relationship with him is really like, where it is going, and how we are being called to live out our time on earth. Lent is an excellent space to use for this deepening of our friendship with God and our commitment to working in partnership with him during the lifetime we are given here.

I hope this Lent course will provide you with the guided space necessary, and enable you to develop both God-awareness and self-awareness, so that both individually and corporately your faith is deepened, renewed and refreshed.

The idea of a spiritual journey from the city into the desert, spending time in the mountains, negotiating the steep-sided wadi and discovering the wellspring water before returning to the city grows out of an inspiring pilgrimage from Nazareth to Bethlehem which I walked in April 2000. In this book the journey has become an imaginary one, with images from deserts, mountains and water drawn from this and many other encounters over the years, but I think you will still sense quite strongly the physical grounding in the Holy Land. It is used as a metaphor, both for our spiritual journey week by week, and also a pattern for the suggested time of prayer, which you may find helpful to use daily on your own and weekly in a group. The pattern is on pages 9-13.

Throughout the chapters for each week there are reflective meditations to follow, and it is quite important that you spend time on these before continuing with the chapter, as I think you will find that the distance travelled in the reflection enables you to get most out of the following sections. There is space provided to make notes, draw or paint your responses to the reflections, as you feel appropriate.

You will sometimes need to use a Bible to accompany this book, and I recommend choosing a version which you can understand and relate to comfortably.

In writing this log book of our journey I am accompanying you, and will be praying for you, that God will use this Lent to reveal to you areas and directions he wants you to notice and address in the process of your deepening friendship with him. May the journey be a time of blessing.

SUSAN SAYERS

A pattern of prayer

Leaving the city . . .

> Be still and know that I am God.
> *Psalm 46:10*

> From everlasting to everlasting you are God.
> *Psalm 90:2*

- Prepare a place of prayer – you might light a candle, use a cross, stones, flowers, a picture, look out of a window at a tree or the sky.

- Be still – make your body physically quiet and still, relaxed but attentive. Breathe evenly.

- 'Know that I am God' – you might say one of the following, holding your breath briefly and then breathing more deeply as you come to the dots to focus on God's presence:

  'The Lord is here . . . His Spirit is with us . . .'

  'Glory be to God who is Father, Son and Holy Spirit; as God was in the beginning . . . is now . . . and shall be for ever. Amen.'

Entering the desert . . .

> Very early in the morning, while it was still dark,
> Jesus got up, left the house and went off to a solitary place,
> where he prayed.
> *Mark 1:35*

> O God, you are my God, earnestly I seek you;
> my soul thirsts for you, my body longs for you
> in a dry and weary land where there is no water.
> *Psalm 63:1*

- Bring to mind all your present areas of concern and responsibility, each matter which keeps nudging you. One by one commit them, and all those involved, to God's keeping. At each one say, 'Let your will be done in this on earth as it is in heaven.'

- Call to mind any outstanding debts you owe – in money, time or forgiveness. Particularly work at forgiving the people who have wronged you or let you down. Recognise where you are in the wrong and ask God's healing and forgiveness. Say, 'Forgive us our sins *as we have forgiven* those who sin against us.'

Spending time in the mountains . . .

O Lord, our Lord,
how majestic is your name in all the earth!
Psalm 8:1

Worship the Lord in the beauty of his holiness.
Psalm 96:9

- Mentally, at least, take off your shoes, because this is holy ground.

- Worship God. You might like to use words such as these:

Blessed be God in the light of the sun
Blessed be God in the rain and wind and all weathers
Blessed be God . . . *continue with your own praises, such as: Blessed be God in the flowers which opened today . . . in the cat's contented purring . . . in my children's playing . . . in the moving cloud shapes . . . in the laws of physics . . . in every argument resolved and every act of kindness . . . in lives well lived . . .*

in shape and colour, sound, taste and touch . . .
And finish: Blessed be God!

- Without saying anything, be very still, simply knowing that your whole life and existence is wrapped in the light of God's presence as you pray.

Negotiating the wadi . . .

Keep me safe, O God, for in you I take refuge.
Psalm 16:1

The Lord upholds all those who fall
and lifts up all who are bowed down.
Psalm 145:14

- Bring to God all those who are in any kind of trouble, sadness or distress . . . 'Lord, have mercy.'

- Bring to God any difficulties or directions you are negotiating, and anything you sense you are hiding from or escaping from . . . 'Christ, have mercy.'

- Bring to God all those whom you love, whether they are still here in the world or have died . . . 'Lord, have mercy.'

Discovering the springs . . .

As the deer pants for the water, so my soul pants for you,
O God. My soul thirsts for God, the living God.
Psalm 42:1-2

The streams of God are filled with water.
Psalm 65:9

I will sing of the Lord's great love for ever!
Psalm 89:1

Because you are my help,
I sing in the shadow of your wings.
My soul clings to you; your right hand upholds me.
Psalm 63:7

- *Either* ask God to give you living water – a spring of water welling up in you to eternal life; *or* thank God for this gift and re-establish in your consciousness the truth of God's indwelling.

- Drink deeply of God's life in yours – his love and compassion, truth, humility and grace . . . 'Because I live, you also will live. On that day you will realise that I am in my Father and you are in me and I am in you.' *John 14:20*

Returning to the city . . .

Blessed are those whose strength is in you.
Psalm 84:4

Teach me your way, O Lord, and I will walk in your truth;
give me an undivided heart, that I may fear your name.
Psalm 86:11

Unless the Lord builds the house, its builders labour in vain.
Psalm 127:1

- Gather up all the prayer of this time in the pattern of prayer Jesus taught his disciples:

'Our Father in heaven, hallowed be your name. Let your kingdom come. Let your will be done on earth as in heaven. Give us today our daily bread and forgive us our sins as we forgive those who sin against us. And lead us not into temptation but deliver us from evil. For the kingdom, the power and the glory are yours for ever and ever. Amen.'

- As you prepare to leave this time of prayer and return to the concerns of the day, know that you are not alone, but equipped with God's life as you live through the day ahead.

  'Send us out in the power of your Spirit to live and work to your praise and glory. Amen.'

1: Entering the desert

As you leave the noises of the city, the silence of the hills creeps out to meet you. In the distance you can see the desert – folded and bleached, growing blue and misty towards the horizon, and stretching wide. As you walk closer, the road system downgrades from tarmac to stones to track, and the vegetation from trees to bushes to low scrub.

You run your hands over the bulky water bottles you are carrying and sense that, though heavy, their weight is vital. You are conscious of adventure, of deliberately stepping out of the city comfort zones and into an untamed landscape where survival does not just happen but must be carefully planned. No longer able to rely on city infrastructures, you are brought in touch with the responsibility of providing for your own life needs in the context of what the landscape provides. At this point of leaving one way of living and entering another, you are made extra aware of all the support the city structures provide to free you up for spending your time on things other than survival.

In contrast the approaching desert looks alarming.

Reflection

The boundary lines have fallen for me in pleasant places.
Psalm 16:6

Think your way through a usual day, noticing everything you are provided with. Be thankful for all the structures of daily living which we normally take for granted. Notice which things and structures you would find it very hard to do without, even for a short time.

We cannot take the city into the desert with us, much as we might like to. Entering the desert is a time for travelling light, paring down to the essentials and meeting ourselves face to face without the city's distractions. Busyness and activity, entertainments and amusements all keep us, most of the time, mercifully occupied so that we can avoid too much raw meeting with ourselves. The desert is a kind of naked place – naked in terms of bare ground, but also reflecting back to us our naked souls which the city helps us keep masked and clothed.

On this journey we are going to try being brave enough to leave the distractions and the masks behind. Our first task is to come to terms with what we cling to. We are like the rich young man who went away sad when Jesus invited him to sell all that he had and give it away, before joining Jesus as a disciple. Why did Jesus' words make him sad? The reason for his sadness was that he possessed so much and had naturally become attached to that way of living. Jesus was calling him to part with the material things he had grown to trust and rely on, so that he could travel light and trust instead in God's providence. It was also an invitation to face up to his own identity without the distractions and masking which his wealth obligingly provided for him. Throughout the gospels we find Jesus displaying this rather uncomfortable tendency to bring people face to face with who they really are. Of course, it is ultimately liberating, but initially the prospect is very like leaving the city and entering the desert. It can be terrifying.

You have thought over the things you are deeply attached to, and thanked God for them, and that is good. A spirit of thankfulness helps protect us against possessiveness of anything, since we get into the habit of delighting in it as privilege and gift, rather than clinging on to it as an assumed right. It is all to do with poverty of spirit.

We are now ready to go deeper into the desert by systematically relinquishing our grip on all we 'have'. That includes things like daydreams and ambitions, hopes, fears, grudges and so on – not just the openly acknowledged ones, but the secret ones we rarely have the courage to admit, even to ourselves. Yes, I know this is immensely uncomfortable – I am trying to do it with you as I write, and already I am flinching at the prospect! But, as I said, the desert is not a comfortable place to enter. It is windswept and bare, but an excellent classroom for the soul. Pray for one another, and for me, as you commit yourselves to this exercise, and I shall be praying for you, that Jesus will draw to your attention the areas he wants you to notice, and that you will have the courage to face them with honesty.

Reflection

Sell all that you own, and distribute the money to the poor, and you will have treasure in heaven; then come, follow me.
Luke 18:22

Set time aside, on a walk perhaps, or regularly throughout the day, to relinquish your grip on and control of all these areas in your life. You are not being asked to turn your back on them – many of these things are good and beautiful – but to come to the place where you are prepared to release them should God ask it of you. You will find this highlights to you the things you cherish most, and the places where your treasure really lies.

Don't just look at possessions; it may be things deeper than that, such as a particular mindset, others' good opinion of you, relationships, ambitions, deep-seated fears and expectations, things from the past which you secretly rather enjoy hanging on to, or projects which you secretly know are turning into empire-building. It is not the things themselves, but our determined grip on them which turns them into possessions, weighs heavily and chains us.

Name these areas and hand them over to God; allow him to take the possessiveness from you.

Well done. You will discover that this is not a 'once and for all' exercise; you may well find that your possessions have somehow crept after you and caught you up as you endeavour to travel light into the desert. But having committed yourself to 'selling your possessions', you will notice when they have caught you up and be more able to unpack them again.

It is strange walking in the Judean desert. This is not a desert of sand, but limestone rock and creamy dust. It feels rather as if you are walking over giant rounded unfired pots. The surface is weathered into patterns of waved ridges, like mudflats at low tide, and in the springtime a faint haze of green appears wherever moisture has allowed some growth. When the sun is low in the sky the patterns are accentuated with shadow.

Climbing to the top of one rounded hill you can see the same landscape stretching away from you in all directions. More rounded hills, more dips and ridged slopes, and a lot of sky. Between the valleys and the tops are the smoothed edges, cracked with caves. The poet W. H. Auden wrote the poem 'In Praise of Limestone' which he begins like this:

> If it form the one landscape that we, the inconstant ones,
> are consistently homesick for,
> this is chiefly because it dissolves in water.

There is something about limestone landscapes which resonates with the human spirit's restlessness. There in rock is the character of adaptability and change set in a form which speaks of the unchanging. Rather like the character of an elderly person's face, etched in the wrinkles, it confronts us with the truth that the shape of our souls is not arbitrary but the inevitable result of accumulated choices in relation to the weathering of each day's experiences.

And this was the setting in which the Son of God, the Messiah, struggled with choices. How was this life's work to be achieved? How were the people to experience Emmanuel – 'God with us'? How was God's reign to be announced and shown to have come?

One of the vital lessons we can learn from Jesus' time in the desert at the start of his ministry is the value of setting time aside for thinking through the overarching and underpinning of all our decision-making. If we don't do this, we may end up making snap decisions off the top of our heads, which we may well later regret.

So what are the overarching and underpinning values which determine our choices and ways of reacting to circumstances? Perhaps we need to look at that on two levels: both what they are, and also what we would like them to be. The two may not necessarily match up!

Reflection

So Lot chose for himself the whole plain of the Jordan
and set out towards the east.
Genesis 13:11

Using situations from your own life in the past week or so, look candidly at the way you have made choices and at all the motives involved in the way you have handled the various situations.

It may help to record these twice – once as they are, and once as we would like them to be – so that you can compare and contrast your findings. Notice the mixture of motives in your decision-making; we all work at many different levels all the time, and it is good to recognise this. Here in the desert we can take the opportunity of the bare landscape to establish (or re-establish) ground rules for all our decisions and choices from now on for the rest of our life here on earth. Every time we are faced with a choice or decision we are exercising our God-given free will. We know from our own personal history, and from the history of the world, that free will is an extraordinarily generous and courageous gift to give, because it is such a perilous, risky and costly one. If we are free to choose then there always has to be the possibility that people will choose evil rather than good, and we do just that, time and again. So fundamental to our chosen way of living as God's children is being attentive students or disciples when it comes to learning how to make good use of that costly gift of free will.

Let's watch Jesus in action to learn the best ground rules of all.

What do you notice about the way Jesus deals with the time of temptation in the desert? Take a few minutes to read it through now with that question in your mind – it's recorded in Matthew chapter 4, Mark chapter 1 and Luke chapter 3. The two things which I particularly noticed this time were the way Jesus uses scripture each time to counter the possibility of wrong decision making, and the way he is so focused on sharing the will of God in every choice. Clearly we can learn from both these methods.

1. Be well fed on the word of God in scripture

Just as we take care over our physical diet, so as to grow strong and maintain health and energy, so we need to feed daily on God's word. For many people the Sunday readings in church are all they 'eat' – imagine trying to make good decisions at work and in relationships if you were trying to survive on one Sunday lunch a week! Regular feeding on scripture is not a luxury item but a basic essential for our life in Christ. As we become really familiar with God's word, his Spirit enables it to take root in our thinking and loving, so that we are far better equipped for the exercise of our free will. I'm not talking about picking verses out of context to throw at those who disagree with us; I mean becoming so steeped in scripture from prayerful reading over the years that we start thinking and seeing with the mind and heart of God.

2. Desire to share the will of God

Closely linked with feeding on the word of God is this focus we naturally see in Jesus of sharing the will of God. The words of scripture Jesus uses in the desert affirm dependence on God, trust in God and obedience to God. All these grow out of a longing and commitment to live every aspect of our lives with reference to God's will. No wonder Jesus taught his disciples to pray 'Let your kingdom come – let your will be done on earth as it is in heaven'. Free will exercised in the context of wanting to share God's will means making choices and decisions which are in harmony with God's nature and wish.

Our journey this week . . .

. . . has had us appreciating what we have, and then deliberately leaving non-essentials behind and travelling light into a place of bareness to encounter God and our real selves. In the desert we have looked at the way we make our choices and measured that up against the teaching model of Jesus.

Loving Father,
in the context of this desert place
we can see more clearly our need of you
and our frequent, wilful neglect of that need.
Establish us in the depth of our being as your people,
and give us the grace to learn from you
what this means for us in our lives.
Give us both the courage and the desire
to pray that your will may be done on earth
as it is in heaven;
that your will may be done in us on earth
as it is in heaven.
Amen.

In a group . . .

Share what you have discovered about yourselves and about society through travelling light and entering the desert.

Work together on a picture or banner, expressing these insights using collage, paint, drawing or graphics.

2: Spending time in the mountains

The main thing I am initially conscious of in mountain country is how fit I'm not! My whole body protests at the gradients, one of my knees reminds me of an accident I once had, and my lungs and heart work extra hard to cope with my mind's choice to be here scrambling up steep rocky places. Sometimes the narrow ledges and huge drops scare me. There are times when I wonder why I ever chose to come here and put myself through this when I could be lying on a beach somewhere exercising only my right arm to bring the odd drink to my mouth or smooth in more suncream.

But get to any viewpoint and I know exactly why I'm here. It's a combination of height, space, distance, isolation and beauty which recharges me and re-establishes perspectives and priorities. Humans in the mountains have to recognise their littleness and their vulnerability, the majesty and vastness of creation, and the present moment focused in the landscape of ancient rock and sky. Set apart from all the everyday activity of the lower ground, we can see its limits, limitations and overall pattern and context.

It's not surprising to find that mountains have often been thought of as the dwelling places of gods, or as holy places where people can meet with God. The difficulty of approach is all part of this – it isn't quite the same to arrive at the summit by cable car. Physically we are 'set apart' and 'set above' when spending time in the mountains, and the very word 'holiness' is to do with being set apart and therefore special and different from the ordinary and everyday.

The Bible often links mountains and holiness. We think of Mount Horeb (or Sinai), on whose slopes Moses was drawn apart to investigate the constantly burning bush and found there a meeting with God. It was to Mount Horeb – the sacred mountain – that Moses returned with all the people of Israel, newly rescued from slavery in Egypt, and here that the Law was given, accompanied by thick darkness, flashes of lightning and claps of thunder. The prophet Elijah was led to the holy mountain to talk with God at a crisis in his life – the place where he discovered God not in the powerful wind or fire or earthquake but in 'the still, small voice'. It was after climbing to the top of a mountain that Jesus was transfigured, and seen talking with both Moses and Elijah about his imminent death.

Reflection

Take off your sandals –
the ground where you are standing is holy.
Exodus 3:5

For your next prayer time, take off your shoes and pray in your bare feet. Use the action of unclothing your feet as an outward sign that you are deliberately choosing to 'stand in God's presence'. Read the account of Moses encountering God on Mount Sinai – Exodus 3:1-15.

As soon as Moses comes close to the burning bush, God speaks. He establishes close relationship but at the same time emphasises to Moses his otherness, or the holiness which separates them. So on the holy mountain Moses is shown both God's immanence and his transcendence, and both are important in our understanding of who God is and what he is like. There needs to be a right balance between the familiar close friendship we can have with God and the awe-inspired wonder as we worship him. Spending time in the mountains restores some of that natural awe and wonder which over-familiarity with the 'church services' of worship can sometimes erode.

The truth is, of course, that all of heaven and all of earth are *full* of God's glory, and from time to time we need to make a point of noticing it all over again. So many miracles of creation go unrecognised. Take something as obvious as the sky, for instance. The most dramatic artwork is spread out there in front of our eyes, a constantly changing process of shape and colour, light, texture and perspective. Yet most of the time we hardly lift our eyes to heaven, let alone praise God in the beauty and glory of his creation shining above us.

Part of the mountain experience is to renew our sense of wonder at God's glory all around us, so that we relearn the child's appreciation of our God-given habitat, giving him thanks and praise as a way of life. First of all you will need to make a deliberate point of engaging in this constant praise and thanksgiving, because most of us have simply forgotten that wisdom and lost the habit of wonder. But after a while of walking through each day with our eyes open to notice God's glory, we will find the habit of wonder refreshed in us, and with it a deep-seated hope and joy quite unrelated to other circumstances.

Moses was to go in God's name and authority, and lead God's people out of their slavery and on to this same mountain where they would all worship. Sure enough, plagues and miracles later, we find the people of Israel with Moses in Exodus 19, approaching the holy mountain and preparing to meet there with their God who has rescued them and led them this far on their journey – both a journey to freedom and a journey to become God's holy people.

We too are on a journey to freedom and to becoming God's holy people. Taking the mountain as a holy place where we are drawn to approach the majesty and glory of God, we continue our journey from the desert to the slopes of the mountain. Travelling light, we are getting familiar with the truth of our vulnerability, and our dependence for life itself on the good will of our Creator and Sustainer. Without the distractions of the city, we are experiencing an encounter with our real selves in this raw, uncompromising landscape, where the bare rock offers no cover. So it is in humility and in our need of God and his touch on our lives, that we approach the holiness of the mountain top and wait. God is not to be rushed or controlled. We cannot burst into his presence with our demands, but simply place ourselves in his presence and wait attentively.

Reflection

For you created my inmost being;
you knit me together in my mother's womb.
Psalm 139:13

Practise sitting or kneeling completely still.

Relax your body and get into a position which is comfortable and sustainable. Close your eyes. Stop all movement.

You will start to notice your body's movement of breathing and heartbeat. They are your physical life support. Let them remind you that ultimately God is your life support. Think of God's loving heart beating for you so that you live, and his Spirit breathing into you so that you have his life in yours.

'God is Spirit,' Jesus told the Samaritan woman at Jacob's well, 'and those who worship God must be led by the Spirit to worship him in truth' (John 4:24). It is God himself who draws us to worship and pulls our spirits by his Spirit into his holiness. Sometimes, long before they would call themselves believers, people are aware of this magnetism and find themselves being drawn to seek God's presence even though they have little idea why they are visiting churches, picking up the Bible or asking difficult questions. Often this 'climbing' stage of the search shows in forceful arguing against the faith and aggressive reactions to those who claim to believe. We need to pray particularly for anyone we meet who behaves in this way, as they may well be reacting to a much stronger, invisible invitation from the living God. I have been in that place myself, and it was eventually alone on a mountain that I discovered the holiness and truth of God which I could no longer battle against.

As committed believers, we still need to remain conscious of this truth – that it is God's Spirit within us which draws us towards him and enables us to commune with him. I suppose we are so used to being able to control things in the city that it takes a wilderness situation to remind us that ultimately we are not in control very much at all. True, we have invented machines with things we call 'controls' so that we can negotiate a car in a tight space (well, some of us can!), organise an oven temperature, regulate the air inside a plane, decide when to be woken in the morning, when to have light and when our tomatoes will ripen. All this affects our mindset, so that we become enveloped in a kind of 'control button theology' where we decide when we want godly moments of holiness, and simply press the 'God switch' whenever we want some intervention or comfort.

Of course, it is breathtakingly arrogant to think like this, but because we are all inevitably influenced by our surroundings, and we spend most of our time in 'tame the wild' surroundings, we naturally tend to include God among the wild which we tame, and protest whenever God doesn't fit in with what we'd really like him to be and do.

Here in the mountains of God's holiness it is very different. Conscious of our littleness, in the wild, unpredictable and powerful presence of God, we know ourselves for what we are – human and mortal, and not gods, in the presence of the One who is immortal, Creator, Redeemer, Sustainer, always present, always good. The Holy One. Our very being is cradled in the mind and heart of this awesome being we know as God.

Reflection

Elijah, why are you here?

Read the story of Elijah travelling into the desert as we have done, and on to the mountain of God. It's in 1 Kings 19:1-13.

As you read, imagine the journey, the terrain and the experience as if you are watching it in a film.

So we seek him and desire to know him as he knows us. We desire to know ourselves as he knows us. We climb the steep rocky places that will bring us closer to his holiness, only to find that our climb is itself his gift – his way of drawing us lovingly into a closer relationship with him. And that's how it was for Elijah, spent and exhausted, and running for his life. Instinctively he heads for the holy mountain and discovers God coaxing him on his way with shelter, sleep, food and drink provided for the journey. On the mountain he finds a cave and creeps into it, almost as if he is in one of the creases in the palm of God's hand. God, in his otherness and holiness, is not seen but Elijah knows he is in the right place, tucked up in God's presence, and waiting on God to reveal himself.

The really important thing about praying is nothing to do with words, but deliberately seeking out the company of God. All prayer is simply spending time in God's company. Sometimes this will take the form of conversation, with both listening and speaking going on. At other times there will be no words at all, but a sense of companionship, or peace; of almost tangible Presence; of empowering, or challenging self-knowledge which leads us to repentance and new freedom. These are the times in which our relationship with God deepens and grows, so naturally the more we are consciously in God's company, the closer we will get and the greater will be our love for him. Like any human relationship, regular contact is essential.

As we, like Elijah, spend time on the slopes of the holy mountain of God, we are learning about the principle of prayer as relationship. Not so much something we do as something we are. Being God's people means living and breathing his life in our own and our life in his. So what happens when we tuck ourselves into the rock of God's love and wait for him to reveal himself? Again, we can learn from the mountains.

Imagine sheltering in a mountain cave during a thunderstorm. First there is the gradual darkening sky with the distant rumble of thunder, and the wind rising. Birds are unsettled and the wind is fitful and gusting, noisy and threatening. Lightning flashes and there is that tension in the counted seconds before the thunder crashes. Drops of rain fall separate and distinct, like an announcement, before the full storm reaches us.

Quite suddenly the sky discharges huge quantities of water, slapping down on the rock at speed so that it bounces back up and makes the wet surface churn and boil. Brilliant light splits the sky again and again, and the air thunders as it races in to reclaim the vacuum. The noise ricochets from one rock face to another, surrounding us in its reverberation.

Makeshift rivers and streams scramble to leave the heights, excitedly taking the shortest routes. One flash of lightning splits apart a huge rock, and, as the thunder roars in, shattered fragments and huge boulders rattle and crash.

The storm sometimes moves around in circles in the mountains, veering away and charging in again until it is spent and quietens to a whisper. The calm after a violent storm is a washed and radiant calm, with the air's clarity like spring water, the light vibrant, the rock silent and still. If we were to call it peace, it would be more like the Jewish 'shalom' – full and complete, with everything settled and whole.

It was this kind of moment in the mountains when God entered into conversation with the waiting Elijah. Quietly and insistently God asked him a question: 'What are you doing here, Elijah?' It was exactly the same question he had asked him before, and Elijah had poured out his misery and despair into the listening ear of God. So what is different this time around, and why does God ask the same question?

The important difference is that between the first question and the second, Elijah had witnessed the power and glory of God in creation, so that the ground had shifted not only in the earthquake but in Elijah's perception of the problem as well. As Mother Julian was shown, 'and all manner of things shall be well' in the context of God's presence. As Jesus reassured his disciples, 'with God all things are possible'. When we bring our impossible problems and heartaches to God in the mountains of his holy presence, and wait there in his company, we shall gradually see them in the context of his power and love, so that they are no longer the devastating hopeless situations we brought with us, but are transformed, partly through the transformation of our own perception.

Our journey this week . . .

. . . has taken us into the awe and wonder of God's holy presence and the recognition of his glory all around us in earth and heaven. In the mountains we have discovered the value of stillness and waiting on God, and seen prayer as privileged relationship with the awesome God of creation.

Lord God of power and humility,
in whom we live and on whom we depend,
heal these eyes of mine
that I may see with your integrity and compassion.
Drawn by your Spirit within me,
may I spend more time in your company from now on,
learn to be still in your presence,
and worship you in spirit and in truth.
Amen.

In a group . . .

Share memories and photos of places in the world where you have been made particularly aware of God's glory.

Talk over anything you noticed on this week's reading of the encounters Moses and Elijah had with God.

Photo: Revd Andrew Ashdown

3: Negotiating the wadi

Wadi are those deep, steep-sided rocky ravines in the desert which take the flash floods racing down from the mountains and become dry and parched in summer. They have got into the habit of doing this for such a long time that the force of water has sliced through layers and layers of rock, so in places it feels less like a valley and more like a long open-topped cave. Making our way down a wadi is like negotiating a dry riverbed, as the ravine floor is strewn with pebbles and huge boulders. Sometimes, where the floodwater has taken a short cut, the rock sheers suddenly away from us and presents us with one of those breathtaking views down-valley, before we pick our way carefully down the rock to the new, lower stage of the wadi floor. Often there is a narrow ledge path worked into one of the steep rock sides, so that the sky is small and distant above and the wadi floor small and distant below.

The deep floor is mainly in shadow, apart from midday, and in places you can tell where pools from the rains have lingered as plants are growing. Flowers colonise any crevice where moisture can gather and small furry animals waddle purposefully around. In the wadi walls are caves and overhangs, and early Christians used to come and live the hermit life here.

I wouldn't want to negotiate a wadi alone, and in the Bible they are often described as places of darkness and danger, though also of refuge and hiding from enemies. We think of Psalm 23, for example – 'Though I walk through the valley of the shadow of death I will fear no evil, for you are with me, your rod and your staff give me comfort.' As a traveller in such a valley of shadows and darkness and possible hidden dangers from flash floods, accidents and attack, companions are of great comfort and help.

As we journey through the wadi we will need each other. In a practical way, we will be helping each other round, over and through the huge jumble of boulders, and past the eroded gaps in the narrow ledges. We can share the carrying of food and water, and encourage each other where anyone is fearful or tired. We can enjoy the landscape together and share the times of eating, resting and praying.

Reflection

The Lord is my shepherd; there is nothing more I shall need.

Read Psalm 23.

Think over a time when you have been in a situation of physical, spiritual or emotional difficulty, and have been helped through it. Thank God for the help received.

Now think of those you know who are at the moment negotiating difficult terrain in their life. In God's company draw alongside them and pray for them.

As Christians we need to travel together, helping and upholding one another, encouraging and affirming one another in faith and godly living, and sharing the times of joy and celebration. Since we are a faith community, it is part of our calling to be bound together in God's love. Negotiating the wadi together can teach us this about our shared adventure.

Spiritually speaking, there are plenty of huge boulders and areas of uneven and dangerous ground to encounter on our way. Never did Jesus promise his followers a pain-free, hassle-free environment. Rather the opposite, in fact. He sent the seventy disciples out 'as sheep among wolves', warned them that they would meet abuse and persecution on account of the gospel, and told a would-be follower that the Son of Man 'had nowhere to lay his head'. Another time Jesus told his disciples, 'If any of you want to be my followers, you must take up your cross and follow me. If you want to save your life, you will destroy it. But if you give up your life for me, you will find it.'

None of that sounds terribly inviting, and we know from Luke's account of the early Church in his book of Acts that Jesus' warnings were very necessary. Paul catalogues a fearsome range of dangerous situations and insults which have happened to him as a direct result of preaching the gospel, and Acts recounts many episodes of stone-throwing, imprisonment, aggressive accusations, and narrow escapes from death, all linked with following Jesus. You can imagine the possible job descriptions for the Christian life when it comes to payment and occupational hazards. On the face of it, it is hard to imagine anyone applying to join up.

Many people assume that today and in our society all that has changed, and we can enjoy the positives of being a Christian without the dangers and discomforts. Certainly we are, locally, immensely blessed in the way we are free to express our faith in Jesus without risking our lives, our employment or our children's places at university. But as Church – community and worldwide – many of us are indeed suffering such torture and persecution. As followers of Christ and members of Christ's Body we can no more disassociate ourselves from those who are suffering for their faith than we can live an independent existence as a big toe or an armpit. When one member suffers the whole body suffers, and we are called to support and encourage one another. Not just those in our own particular locality, but all those of the whole household of faith, standing up with them for justice and mercy, and speaking for them wherever the oppressed have no voice.

Otherwise it is like watching one member of our group in the wadi falling on the rock or trapped, and doing nothing at all to help them.

Will such action make us popular with oppressive governments or even with our neighbours at home? Probably not. Probably we will find ourselves becoming a bad smell in people's nostrils. But risk is part of the Christian calling because it is impossible to take seriously the summary of the Law without it. As soon as we take on board the commands to love God with heart and mind and soul and strength, and to love our neighbour as we love ourselves, the risks are already built in by default, and cannot be erased. It is impossible to love God and others without becoming perceived as enemies to some. It's perfectly possible to choose a select few to love so that we stay rich and popular, of course, but unfortunately 'loving our neighbour' doesn't allow us the luxury of such comfortable limiting. As Christians we are to love everyone as we love ourselves.

The drive to survive means that we love ourselves primarily in a very practical way. We check that we are adequately fed and clothed, ensure that we are safe and getting good healthcare and education, and pamper ourselves with occasional treats. We have these long trained cranes sticking out of our shoulders to hoist food to our mouth and bring scatches to any itch. A commitment to love others as we love ourselves is therefore bound to involve us in practical care, noticing needs and difficulties and working to alleviate them as a matter of urgency. Significantly, Jesus taught his disciples to pray 'give *us* this day *our* daily bread', so that whenever we pray the Lord's prayer we are reminded of this teaching to love others as we love ourselves.

Reflection

I have set you an example.
John 13:15

Read the account of Jesus washing his disciples' feet, and teaching them through this the kind of loving service they are to take as their model. You'll find it in John 13:4-17.

Imagine yourself in that upper room as Jesus comes to wash your feet as well. Let him wash them and notice how you feel about that. Now imagine yourself washing the feet of those who might normally 'serve' you or look after your needs.

Photo: Revd Andrew Ashdown

We who profess to follow the way of love must love professionally. By that I don't mean anything detached or contrived for what we can get out of it. I mean that all our behaviour must match up with what we claim to believe, so there is no gap between the talk and the walk. That probably sounds incredibly obvious, and perhaps we feel we are doing it already. But it's one of those things we need to check regularly and rigorously. As a company of people whose identity comes directly from the God of love, justice and mercy, the Church should be recognisable by the loving way its members live. We ought to be a by-word for action which is full of generosity and thankfulness, mercy and forgiveness. Are we?

Just as thankfulness is a habit, so too, as we discovered in the mountains, is kindness and loving care of one another – not because we like someone or find them attractive as people, but because they too are children of God, created and sustained by his love. It's not the grand one-off acts so much as the far more costly loving-habit which matters. Can I suggest one or two areas we as church need to check this habit of love?

• Does our idea of welcoming people stop at the smile and greeting, or is it prepared to go as far as real relationship?

• Do the conversations before and after the service speak of generous love and acceptance, or is there a decided slant towards the negative grumble mode?

• What happens when someone becomes ill or too frail to come to church on their own? Are members of the church family looking after their needs, popping in to visit and so on?

• Are there people in your church whose names you don't know yet?

As well as caring for one another's practical needs, we are to help and encourage one another in the faith, and that is just as important and can be just as easily overlooked. Sadly I hear too often stories of people who have been attending church for months but never felt accepted; Christians who haven't felt able to talk about their doubts or temptations or need of God's forgiveness with others in church because they are all perceived to be so confident and 'sorted'. Often when a crisis happens in a church it doesn't just happen out of the blue but can be traced back to a series of worrying symptoms which have not been addressed and so allowed to fester.

- Do church members pray together regularly?

- Is there a network of spiritual encouragement and support in groups close enough and small enough for problems and doubts to be picked up and worked through before things get out of hand?

- And are there structures in place to protect these small groups from becoming oases for discontent and unhealthy cliques?

- Are spiritual mentors encouraged for all ages, so that we are helping one another's faith to develop?

Travelling out in challenging terrain, we wouldn't dream of setting off without adequate support structures, and ensuring that all members are properly equipped; spiritual terrain is likewise challenging and requires similarly rigorous support. On our route through the wadi we are likely to be challenged by times of spiritual confusion or panic; times when changes to tradition feel as if the ground beneath us suddenly drops away; times when we must pick our way carefully through the ethical boulders, or past the doubts of eroded pathways.

Many of the psalmists and hymn writers have picked up on the imagery of our life and faith development as a challenging journey, rather than a gentle stroll:

'Lead us, heavenly Father, lead us o'er the world's tempestuous sea'

'Guide me, O thou great Redeemer, pilgrim through this barren land'

'My footsteps hold fast to the ways of your law, in your paths my feet shall not stumble' (Psalm 17)

'Those who go through the desolate valley will find it a place of springs, for the early rains have covered it with pools of water' (Psalm 84)

'The Lord will hold your hand, and even if you stumble you shall not fall headlong' (Psalm 37)

Reflection

Choose one of the phrases opposite to meditate on (or chew on). Write it out clearly and put it down in front of you.

Get settled and still, as before, and then work on the words, allowing them to become re-hydrated in your imagination, mind and heart to a real experience.

Read over and over, slowly, sometimes as a whole phrase, sometimes word by word, so that its meaning is released to your spiritual understanding.

Jesus taught that it would be easy to fall into temptation and hard to avoid that. He was anxious that his disciples should be actively praying in Gethsemane, so that they would be strengthened to resist temptation. He himself was praying desperately as a matter of life and death; it was there in the dark garden that Jesus battled with the powerful temptation to side-step the agony of the crucifixion, and received the courage and strength to accept obedience, even to death on a cross.

Yet we often have an extraordinarily casual approach to temptation which is quite different from what Jesus teaches. It is as if we set off down the wadi on our own, in fashion footwear, lavishly sprinkling bait for the wild animals as we go, and with wads of money poking out of our back pockets to encourage the thieves. And then, when temptations are upon us, we resign ourselves indulgently to giving in to them because we haven't any strength or equipment for fighting against them. The fact that Jesus took temptation so seriously is surely a good reason for us to wake up to its dangers and the good sense of venturing out suitably equipped.

As I have said, travelling together is vital, looking out for each other's needs, praying together and supporting one another through encouraging the good and discerning the dangerous. If, in the wadi, we see a companion placing their weight on a stone which we can see is about to break away from the rock, wouldn't we warn them and point out a more trustworthy route? So why is it that so often we will hold back from pointing out spiritual dangers, and let our companions in Christ go ahead and take dangerous steps which can be devastating for them and for the community?

Sometimes I wonder if, in the name of love and acceptance, we are actually unkind to one another by holding back from talking over our concerns. We need both the grace to accept challenges and warnings from one another, and also the grace to give those challenges and warnings when necessary, not judgementally, but honestly and respectfully.

Reflection

Watch and pray, so that you will not fall into temptation.
Luke 22:46

Take this opportunity to pray that you will not fall into temptation in the days ahead. Pray God's powerful presence into the situations which you know are likely to be difficult – perhaps times of tiredness and hunger, or hormones; situations or relationships in which you recognise the temptation to jealousy or resentment, selfishness or boasting.

Ask God to strengthen you in situations where you perhaps feel threatened and are likely to react defensively or aggressively; ask him to give you more love in a difficult relationship.

Thank God for this opportunity to pray and prepare, ahead of the temptations, and ask him to equip you for tackling the danger zones.

Finally, negotiating the wadi can teach us about being lost and found. Sin in our lives can lead us down some deep narrow ravines which gradually become more treacherous. We may feel trapped, knowing we need to climb back up, but afraid of that backtracking at the same time as hating the precarious place we are in.

This is where the image of Jesus as the Good Shepherd is wonderfully encouraging. We can know that as soon as the bleats of our misery and longing reach Jesus' ears, the Shepherd will have set out to find us. We will not be abandoned to struggling back on our own; the Good Shepherd will come and free us, either leading us carefully back to safety or lifting us up on his shoulders and carrying us there. That is his promise, a promise we can trust, no matter how far off the wadi path we have stumbled, and how long we have been stubbornly continuing in the wrong direction. There is such relief, joy and hope at being found by Jesus that it is well worth bleating, however impossible it seems that anyone might want to bother with rescuing us. Everyone who wants to be found will be found.

Our journey this week . . .

. . . has taken us through the steep-sided wadi, realising our need of one another's companionship in the faith journey. This is important both for the practical caring love and also the mutual encouragement and support in our growing relationship with Jesus. We have explored our need of prayerful preparation in dealing with temptation and been reminded of Jesus' promise to come and find us whenever we are lost.

You, O Lord, are the Good Shepherd,
leading your people safely
through the steep, rocky valleys
as well as the green pastures.
Teach us to love one another as you love us,
looking out for one another's needs,
helping one another through the difficult places
and warning one another of dangers.
Thank you that when we lose our way
and are unable to free ourselves from sin,
you set off with your rod and staff
to find us and bring us back to safety.
Amen.

In a group . . .

Share your thoughts about the world church's calling to be a community of love. Discuss the practical implications of this.

Try expressing in art, clay or movement, what 'Lead us not into temptation' means to you.

4: Discovering the springs

We had to carry our water with us into the desert. It was necessary to keep drinking to avoid dehydration. One of those blissful moments in a hot, dry landscape is coming across a deep rocky well. There is a large flat slab of stone over it and a rocky sink carved out beside it into which the water can be poured for the animals to drink. The bucket is let down a long way – perhaps 8-10 metres – into the silent darkness before a distant splash echoes upwards, as the bucket hits the hidden underground stream or pool.

Around the well is a trodden area of mud, covered in the prints of all the creatures drawn to its gift of water. We, too, can drink deeply, and pour it over one another's heads and shoulders, cold, clear and wonderfully refreshing. These ancient wells have supported life here for thousands of years and without them it is impossible to survive. What arrogant cruelty it is to cement or blow them up and pass the death sentence on whole communities, histories and ecostructures. Tragically in the Holy Land today we are as likely to find wells illegally choked with cement as free flowing and clear, in a bid to rationalise the takeover of Palestinian land.

Thankfully, Elijah's spring still bubbles up out of the ground without even the need for plunging a bucket down beneath the surface of the ground. Even in summer it bubbles up, spilling out of the rock at the lower end of a wadi into a wide, welcome pool. Plants grow around the edges – a few trees shade one end of it, and it is sheer luxury after negotiating the dry wadi to splash and paddle about in this flowing, living water. It has its own song of life which the birds seem to imitate, and deep in our human psyche there is another song – a memory of instinct – that calls profoundly to us of survival, life and security, of sustenance and hope. Jesus talked of himself as 'living water' as the Samaritan woman drew water from Jacob's well, near her own town. Jesus said that the one who drinks from this water shall never again be thirsty. He talked of making a well spring up inside us, so that we will always have the source of clear, life-giving water welling up from deep within us.

Reflection

If you do away with the yoke of oppression, with the pointing
finger and malicious talk . . . the Lord will guide you always;
he will satisfy your needs in a sun-scorched land and will
strengthen your frame. You will be like a well-watered garden,
like a spring whose waters never fail.
Isaiah 58:9-11

Think about the way a never-failing stream and a well-watered
garden bless people who come to them. That is how we are to
be – a source of blessing to those needing spiritual refreshment.

Let God show you the areas in which you are already such a
blessing, and the places where as yet you are not.

It's such an amazingly refreshing and energising thought that we are not
only invited to drink deeply of God's living water, but also to be transformed into living water wells ourselves, so that we become places of
refreshment, life and blessing for others. And we can see from our
experience of other people how necessary this is. Think of those people
at your church in whose company you feel refreshed and enabled, who

make you want to have a friendship with God which gives you what it is obviously giving them.

Those who oppress, point the finger and talk maliciously have the effect of flattening us, squashing hope and enthusiasm, and making us 'dry up'. Place that in the context of a church community and you can see its devastating effect on the life of a church: it is like cementing a well.

As we arrive on our journey at this lively, bubbling spring of water, we are going to drink deeply and be transformed by it, so that we as individuals – and we as church – become places where a spring of water wells up to eternal life. A place where people will be attracted to come as the Samaritan woman was – 'Sir, give me this water!' Those in whom God's living water wells up are noticeably attractive. They have something about them – a secret of life – which others want and are drawn to.

People describe it as a naturalness and fullness of life which doesn't seem worn down by the usual pressures; as a lightness of heart which is comfortable and unaffected, encouraging and unshockable, appreciative of God's blessings, patient when things go wrong and somehow secure so that the person is not generally defensive. The essence of all this is that it is real and cannot be mimicked. It flows naturally or not at all. It means that since we can never set out to acquire it by working from the behaviour end, there's no point in wearing ourselves out trying hard to act the part. This is a great relief, but how, then, can we change ourselves into wellsprings?

We can't. We can only *be changed*. This is a work which God does in us, by virtue of being invited into our lives, because you can't have the living God dwelling anywhere without his presence showing. It is good news for all of us that while we cannot transform ourselves, however conscientious or organised we might be, we *can* be transformed by God living in the depth of our living. At this point let me reassure you regarding something which scares people. They are wary of inviting God that close for fear that his presence will somehow obliterate the person they are and know and, for all its faults, love. Well, God will not take away a scrap of what we are, or alter our genetic make-up. We need not worry that this indwelling is like a takeover bid. On the contrary, Jesus living within us actually enables us to be more who we really are.

Perhaps you have sometimes collected stones and shells from rock pools or the shallow water's edge, and find they lose their brightness once they're dry. It is when they are lying there in the clear, moving water that they look particularly beautiful. It's rather like that with us – Jesus' living water sets our real selves shining.

Reflection

Then I shall put my Spirit into you and you will come to life.
Ezekiel 37.14

Find a cold stone and hold it in the palm of your hand. As the stone warms to your blood heat, think of God's love warming your life with his life-blood heat as he holds your life in the palm of his hand.

As with stones on the bed of a stream, we are all different, not only in appearance but also in composition and character. One of the lovely things about paddling around in the shallows is picking up so many different kinds of pebble, all of which, like us, are on a journey, this place being their present resting place. They have come from the molten core of the earth, been fastened for millions of years in mountains, broken off by earthquakes and erosion, transported by rivers and glaciers, and now, for a while, settled in the water of this pool, or in the palm of your hand. Pebbles humble us with their timescale and travelling, reminding us of our own rich diversity and our transience.

Our time on earth is a section of our existence, but not the whole of it. When we invite the living God to dwell in our living, we are inviting entrance to a new dimension completely. We call God 'the living God' because his identity and characteristic is to be always alive. He refers to himself as 'I AM'. Let's explore that name and see what it can teach us about God. Think for a moment of what you would be saying about yourself if you gave your name as 'I AM'. Can you see how it expresses constant vigorous life, unlike anything we know of human life which is all about beginnings and ends, birth and death? 'I AM' places God outside those limits which are our own natural habitat, so that we recognise straightaway God's difference from us. If God's existence is not governed by words like 'before' and 'after', if he is at any moment totally alive and present, we can understand that God's perspectives are going to look different from our time-shackled perspectives.

Just as we might watch a beetle in the grass and know that it can have no grasp of the wider world we relate to, so, faced with the constant and eternally living God, we have to recognise our limitations as humans and time-dwellers. This is called mortality, and the knowledge of our 'start and finish' habitat affects the way we think and feel and live. Our mortality is one of the hardest things for us to accept, and we are always trying desperately to cheat the system.

Imagine the effect, then, of having living within our time-bound life the life of God, with its perspective of immortality and 'alive for ever' quality. Imagine how that will have the power to liberate us from all kinds of worries and pressures which are driven ultimately by death avoidance – or perhaps I should say oblivion avoidance. For instance, if the material world is the full extent of our existence, there is enormous pressure to acquire wealth and status within those terms of reference. From our mortality perspective these are vitally important. Likewise it is natural to worship youth and vitality as furthest from the end point of death, and so, not surprisingly, millions are spent on products to stave off or mask the ageing process. There is an urgency about experiencing as much of this 'life' as possible, with a ready market in all the heightened experience substances and thrills. There is the cruel disappointment of plans failing to work out, ideals and dreams for the short time available shattered or less satisfying than had been hoped. There is the urgency to prolong this physical life as long as possible, at any cost, as if death were the greatest enemy of all.

But if we recognise our mortality as part of our God-given human identity, is death the arch-enemy we make it? St Francis actually referred to it as Sister Death.

We are so used to the furnishings of this death-driven perspective that even as Christians, supposedly believing in life after death, they influence us, dulling our joy, chaining us up and preventing us from living the new life of freedom in Christ with his life bubbling up within us. One of the greatest temptations has always been to take on the spiritual truths of the cultures around us. And what is that called? Idolatry.

We need washing clean of all that; we need our spiritual thirst quenching with the satisfying pure water of God's Spirit; we need the living water welling up inside our life and life-style, mindset and values, even at the risk of being thought different from those around us. Of course we will be different! We are to be in the world but not of the world.

Reflection

I no longer live, but Christ lives in me.
Galatians 2:20

Think over the way in which your thinking and values are affected by the values and beliefs of the culture in which you live. Where is that subtly or clearly at variance with our values and beliefs as Christians?

Here at the spring we can let God's living water do its cleansing, healing and refreshing work. Like the water in the membrane sack protecting us on our nine-month journey to birth – our entry into this mortal life we know – God's living water surrounds us and bathes us protectively on our journey to spiritual birth – our entry into immortal life. Not eternal life as a 'next phase' which only starts at death, but life of the God-dimension lived both simultaneously now, and also uninterrupted by death, except in so far as death brings us even more fully into God's presence.

So it isn't something we have to wait until after death to experience, as is often supposed. Rather, our life powered by the water-spring of God's life enables us to experience even death in a new way, just as Francis discovered it to be. This one certainty of our existence here is like a sister, a natural and essential truth of our humanity. When God gives us new life, he does so within the framework of the mortality of our human nature.

I am well aware, having recently lost my mother through death, that it may jar to speak of death in this affectionate way, when we know it as searing pain, cruel separation and tragedy; when the ache of losing loved ones is sharp and intense, and we protest at the injustice of blighted lives and lives cut tragically short. We may well ask how St Francis could possibly embrace as a sister such an unkind and painful phenomenon.

But Francis had invited the wellspring of God's life into his own life, and that enabled him to perceive truth from God's perspective, into which he was adopted. In humility he knew and accepted our mortality as part of our God-given humanness. He saw that there is consequently much that we, with our time-bound limits, cannot expect to under-stand, and our calling here is to be fully human, not failed immortals. Part of this is the great richness of experience – light and dark, joyful and sorrowful colours woven together in the fabric of our being.

It is all far too deep in meaning for us to be able to analyse and quantify, as the instinctive 'Why?' questions demand. But within the all-encompassing life of God we are shown what we need to see – a God whose love envelops us and grieves with us in all the pain, celebrates with us in all the joy, and chooses to make his home with us in our vulnerability, laying glory aside and sharing with us what we most loathe and curse – death itself. Through Christ transforming death into new life in the resurrection, our whole perspective can be similarly transformed, healed of the endemic threat of annihilation, and freed to live the risen life of heaven even as we walk through our human years.

The time has come for us to allow the wellspring of God's life into the very core of our identity, into the essence of our personhood. We are going to wade into this spring and find it flowing not only around us but through us. It is not something we need to fear in any way because the God of complete goodness and love is wanting it for us, and has drawn us here to receive it. Whether this is the first time you have asked God into your life in this way, or whether you have already known the freedom and joy of his indwelling Spirit, welcome God afresh and receive from him life in all the abundance that he longs to give you.

Reflection

Whoever drinks the water I give him will never thirst.
Indeed, the water I give him will become in him a spring
of water welling up to eternal life.
John 4:13

You may like to stand or kneel or run a bath as you ask God for this living water to quench your thirst and become in you a spring welling up to eternal life.

In your imagination wade into the spring water, so that you choose to step into God's environment of new life. Allow him to bathe you and wash away all that has kept you from him. Holding nothing back, open up your real self to the flowing water of God's love, around and within you.

Enjoy this closeness with the God who loves you, who is living and active now, has always been and always will be.

You are in me and I am in you.
John 14:20

Our journey this week . . .

. . . we have discovered the best water source of all and responded to God's invitation to drink freely of the water of life. We have looked at what that 'life' means and how it can affect our outlook and give us a whole new perspective. We have received from God and been refreshed in mind, body and spirit.

Great Spirit of God,
living within us and in whom we live,
we thank you for the way you lavish your love on us
and always give us so much more than we ask for,
so that your joy and peace fill us to overflowing.
We understand that this wellspring of your life in us
is not for our refreshment only,
but that many may be blessed.
May we cherish this water source
and drink from it often,
so that our lives, immersed in yours,
take on the shine of your brightness
and draw others to find their fulfilment in you.
Amen.

In a group . . .

Spend some time in praise and worship, singing together and praying in twos and threes for one another and for the Church.

Make a picture or banner expressing what you have discovered about the wellspring of God's life in our lives.

5: Returning to the city

We must tear ourselves away from the desert, the mountains, the wadi and the spring because it is time to return to the city. Saying goodbye to such landscapes is always difficult, and as we turn our faces towards the city again we may feel a sense of sadness and regret that we can't spend longer here. Hard as it was initially to adjust ourselves to living more simply and travelling light, we now find ourselves valuing that lightness and flexibility. We always need to prepare ourselves for going back to work after a holiday, and for returning home after a retreat, so it is right and good that we include this preparation and adjustment in the final stage of our journey together.

We are not the same people as when we set out on this journey, because God has been accompanying us and drawing us closer into relationship with him. That transforming, or sanctification, is a process of becoming holy, and the very fact that we have committed ourselves to seeking out God's company like this, and his will for us in our lives, has enabled him to move us further on and heighten our awareness of his presence and influence in our lives.

As we dry our feet from the water at the spring and head down the widening valley back to the city, we know that the peace and space of this landscape we have come to reverence will soon be overtaken with the crowding of city life. Some of that will excite and energise us, and the prospect of being fully involved again gives a spring to our step. We also know there will be the distractions awaiting us, to engage us and perhaps leave little time for developing the relationship with God which our journey through Lent in the desert landscape has made possible.

Reflection

*You did not choose me, but I chose you and appointed you
to go and bear fruit – fruit that will last.*
John 15:16

Pause to get in touch with the calling to live your life more deeply committed to Christ. Focus your attention on the areas of conflict and distraction which you know will be holding you back from this. Commit these areas to Christ's reign, so that his kingdom can come in them. Make yourself available to work co-operatively with God in this, so that you are prepared to be involved in God's outcome.

How are we going to manage this tension between the life of prayer and the life of work and action?

It was St Benedict who spelt out an important truth about the life of a believer – that prayer and work, or action, are really all part of the same thing. We don't have to split our life into compartments where our prayer life is in one place and everything else somewhere different. True, religion is often regarded as a hobby – as, for instance, in those consumer questionnaires we get begged to fill in from time to time. There it is in the 'leisure and hobbies' section and I'm never sure whether to tick it or not. If I don't, I'm slotted into the 'no interest in religion' box, and if I do, I'm agreeing that religion is a hobby – something with which I wholeheartedly disagree! Our friendship with the Star-maker encompasses all our living, our choices, actions and relationships, and that image of Jesus of a spring of water welling up inside us to eternal life clearly establishes the nature of prayer immersed in action and action in prayer.

But what about the practicalities of this? However much we may want to combine them, isn't the reality of normal life that there isn't time for both, and prayer is the usual loser? The alarm or the baby wakes us just in time to wash, dress, grab a slice of toast and race to work. Even those retired and living alone often express surprise at how the various chores and activities fill the day so that prayer time is easily interrupted or squeezed out. As we prepare to return, we have the opportunity to take a look at this imbalance in our lives and make some adjustments.

Let's keep in mind as a basic principle that prayer is relationship. In any human relationship the companionship is often conversation or comfortable silence while you are doing something together – working as colleagues, looking together at the shops, sport or art, listening together to music or another speaker, coping together in challenging situations, and talking over together past events and funny or frightening memories. There are times when one of you is in the role of comforter and the other pours out troubles. There are times of celebrating together and encouraging one another. There are also the occasions of misunderstanding and hurt, when in a good relationship feelings are expressed and the painful truths worked through with love, leading to a deeper understanding and trust.

Reflection

How good and pleasant it is
when brothers live together in unity!
Psalm 133:1

I no longer call you servants . . .
instead I have called you friends.
John 15:15

Think over various good relationships in your life and the way
they have grown and developed. Thank God for them, and also
for what they teach you about prayer as relationship.

Good human relationships seem to me a valuable model for our relationship with God. If we commit ourselves to living our lives in his company, we will find a close relationship developing which is all woven into our daily experiences, rather than being a formal, distant or dutiful extra. There are enormous benefits.

Having God as a constant companion means that burdens dumped on us by others can immediately be shared and the heaviness lifted, even while we are on the receiving end. God's words and discernment will come into our own thinking and feeling which we can immediately pass on in conversation. We will be prompted when to speak and when to shut up and listen, when to challenge and when to reassure; when to offer assistance and when to let the learning come through mistakes and experience. We will find our reactions being coloured by the company we keep, with far greater resources of mercy and forgiveness at our disposal than we would have if left to ourselves.

Another bonus is that our Companion does not only have a love and affection for everyone we are meeting, but also a fondness for us. This means that those of us who tend to be kind to everyone except ourselves will find we are nudged to rest and eat and say 'No' to impossible demands – our Companion is supporting us as well as everyone else!

This kind of prayer is, I imagine, the constant prayer advised by St Paul. We can picture him consciously walking with Jesus into the hostile synagogues, and along the roads between cities. No wonder Peter and John could say to the beggar that they could give him no silver and gold, but the healing of Jesus' touch; they were there in Jesus' company as they walked into the shadow of the temple gate, and so it was with Jesus' love and compassion that they looked straight into the man's eyes and saw both his need and his faith.

How can we introduce people to God if we are not constantly in his company? And, conversely, if we *are* in God's company, how can we avoid introducing people to him? They are bound to meet him through our close relationship. The wellspring of God's life is closer than breathing; our roots plunge down into its depths where they are constantly refreshed and nourished, healed and forgiven. Other pockets of water may entice our roots and temporarily gratify us, but we need to know that these are only temporary, and accept that they may well dry up and let us down. Too often we expect of other treasures and other humans what only God can give. In contrast to these water sources, our strong roots are sunk into the living water which never dries up and will keep us fully alive, and bearing the fruits of the Spirit.

Reflection

He is like a tree planted by streams of water, which yields its fruit in season and whose leaf does not wither.
Psalm 1:3

In God's company recognise the pockets of water which we know give us a sense of security. Rather than renouncing them, acknowledge both their value and their temporary nature. Now become conscious of those strong roots thrusting down into the wellspring which never runs dry.

We will find this habit of constant awareness of being in God's company has another important consequence. Our ongoing and deepening relationship with God will make us desire more formal times of prayer and Bible reading on a regular, daily basis. I know we are often advised to get these sorted and organised first, so that through such regular, formal prayer times we gradually discover the informal constant prayer habit emerging. Certainly this can happen, and if you are the kind of person who can easily discipline yourself, you will find it to be wonderfully true.

But my experience is that for many of us it doesn't work like this. The initial commitment of setting regular time aside for prayer is a great ideal, but, rather like those conversations with strangers in a formal situation, our conversations with a God we hardly know are hard to sustain. All too often the commitment remains only as a good intention, with guilt slipping in and discouragement.

If, on the other hand, we begin with cultivating the habit of being conscious of God accompanying us in all our thinking and doing throughout the day, in quite an informal way, so that we are getting to know God right there in the context of our own home and workplace, relationships and challenging situations, we will find we are developing a deep sense of real companionship with God. We shall be getting to know him as real and present and profoundly relevant. It is this real and personal relationship that will motivate us to establish those vital regular times in each day which we deliberately set aside for prayer and Bible reading, not out of duty to a distant stranger, but joyfully out of a relationship of love.

Just as we are enabled to give up smoking or start eating sensibly or exercising regularly as soon as, deep down, we really desire to, so we shall be enabled to discipline ourselves to a daily time of prayer when our growing awareness of God makes us desire more and more of his presence.

So don't weigh yourself down with unsustainable resolutions as we walk back into the city. Just enjoy walking with Jesus and let him make himself known to you in your daily commitments and learning experiences. Knowing him better and better, you will find yourself loving him more and more. And out of that love will come your response of seeking daily prayer and reading scripture.

As we walk further from the desert and the mountains, and the track begins to upgrade to a dusty tarmac, we may find ourselves turning back and searching the hills for a last glimpse of where we sheltered from the heat of the sun or the violence of the storm; of places where our encounter with God has touched us particularly deeply. These are memories to treasure and look at when you are back in the city. Think of it like looking through your photos, which you can do any time to refresh your memory and remind you that these encounters really happened. Otherwise the danger is that the city's values distort our memories and make us doubt what is true just because it is different and 'unnatural' in worldly terms. Cherish the holy places of your life and use them when circumstances or people are threatening to undermine your faith. They were given to you by God.

The city sights and sounds are closer now and louder. Don't let the city crowd out the desert landscape you carry within you, but rather use this inward place of God's presence to encounter the city in a new way. When Jesus sent his disciples out in pairs he told them to be 'wise as serpents and innocent as doves'; another time his teaching was this: 'Do not be overcome with evil, but overcome evil with good.'

This would be entirely terrifying if we were not equipped and empowered for the task. What makes us able to walk back into the city confidently is that we are equipped. In fact, we're far better than equipped. Certainly God does provide us with gifts like wisdom, discernment, hospitality and the grace to forgive. But more than that he infuses his life into our life, so that we all become 'Christophers' – Christ carriers. We take Christ wherever our feet walk, and open each situation, each place, to the power of God's love.

Reflection

I will not leave you as orphans; I will come to you.
John 14:18

Visualise a situation where the love of Christ is badly needed. When you next walk into this situation, be conscious of the truth that Christ really is there as well. Let his love enfold you and his healing flow into the points of conflict and pain.

At the same time another truth is at work which we can only hope to understand as we think with the God-perspective that we have been given. Not only does God dwell in us so that our feet or our thoughts bring his presence into a situation, but he is also there ahead of us, present already and waiting to welcome us. This means that we are able to discover the living God in every face and voice, and in all creation, not simply in the obviously awesome and beautiful.

Every opportunity for loving service, humility and encouragement is an opportunity to meet the gaze of a loving, foot-washing Saviour. All kinds of possibilities are opened up when God's companions realise this and respond. As Psalm 139 proclaims, 'Even the darkness is not dark to you . . .' So whenever you find yourself in a place of pain or darkness – your own, another's or that of a community – bring into it Christ's compassion and hope, security and peace. This way we will be agents of healing and wholeness for the world God sustains and loves, and we have the rest of our life on earth to live out that calling with joy.

Well, we are nearly there – thank you for your company on this walk. Can we remember one another in prayer this Easter as we celebrate the resurrection? We shall be living the risen life freshly aware of the breathtaking implications of it. Let the risen life not be simply a religious phrase we have grown used to hearing, but an expression vibrant with meaning and personal experience, as the power of God's love breaks into our mortality and sets us free to live in that new immortal dimension, interwoven with our humanness. May we drink again and again of the living water bubbling up in the centre of our being, and carry with us into the busyness and activity of the city the inner peace and tranquillity which comes from the indwelling of the living God.

Our journey this week . . .

. . . we have been preparing ourselves to leave the desert and return to the city, reflecting on the places we have travelled together, with the memories of God's revelation, refreshment and challenge, in this majestic landscape of holiness and inner peace. We have endeavoured to see the experiences we have gained, in the context of normal daily 'city' life, so that we may be able to access this time of withdrawal as an ongoing spiritual resource.

Travel with us, Lord, our God,
into the places where we live and work,
into the conversations and the choices,
the pressures, expectations and routines.
As we return from this desert landscape to the city,
may the holiness of your presence
dwell with us and in us,
and may we dwell not only in our time-bound earthly home,
but in your gracious and eternal love.
Amen.

In a group . . .

Have the artwork from the whole course displayed so that people can walk around recalling the journey while music is playing.

Discuss practical ways of supporting one another in our ongoing spiritual journey.